REBEL WRITERS

THE GENIUS BEHIND THE PEN

VOL I

SARAH CROWNE

WHAT'S GOIN' ON?! SLN PUBLISHING, LLC

Copyright © 2024 by Sarah Crowne

WHAT'S GOIN' ON?! SLN Publishing, LLC

All rights reserved.

No part of this publication may be reproduced, distributed, or transmitted in any form or by any means, including photocopying, recording, or other electronic or mechanical methods, without the prior written permission of the publisher, except as permitted by U.S. copyright law. For permission requests, contact WHAT'S GOIN' ON?! SLN Publishing, LLC at whatsgoinonslnpublishing@gmail.com

This publication is designed to provide accurate information in regard to the subject matter covered. While the publisher and author have used their best efforts in preparing this book, they make no representations or warranties with respect to the accuracy or completeness of the contents of this book and specifically disclaim any implied warranties of merchantability or fitness for a particular purpose. The advice and strategies contained herein may not be suitable for your situation. You should consult with a professional when appropriate. Neither the publisher nor the author shall be liable for any loss of profit or any other commercial damages, including but not limited to special, incidental, consequential, personal, or other damages.

No part of this book may be used or reproduced in any manner for the purpose of training artificial intelligence technologies or systems.

First edition 2024

ISBN (Paperback) 979-8-9910052-3-4

ISBN (e-book) 979-8-9910052-4-1

Library of Congress Control Number: 2024921600

https://sarahcrownebooks.com/

For the movers, the shakers, the dreamers, the artists, the writers, the musicians, the philosophers, the entrepreneurs, the outcasts, the underdogs, the ones that take their power back, pick up the pieces, want to heal and never give up on their dreams. . .

This one's for you.

XOXO

Sarah Crowne

Write till your ink be dry, and with your tears
Moist it again, and frame some feeling line
That may discover such integrity.

— WLLIAM SHAKESPEARE

A WRITER'S ADVENTURE

I was itching for an adventure. I just didn't know it yet.

The idea of an adventure stirs something deep within our soul. It's the journey that calls to us. Challenges us. Creates us. Shapes us into becoming something new.

We often imagine that "going on an adventure" means we must travel to distant places and do spectacular things. Slay dragons. Find lost treasures. Solve the mysteries of the universe. No wonder Bilbo Baggins wasn't interested. Staying home in a hobbit hole to eat a homemade dinner, at least to me, sounds better. Safer.

Thankfully, for those of us that are a little more cautious, not all adventures need to be grand or extraordinary. Countless adventures have happened in only a few square miles. In fact, people have lived entire lives and experienced countless stories without traveling far.

Stories are adventures. As a writer, I care a lot about story. Our lives are full of them. Each experience in our lives is like turning a new page, taking us deeper into the chapter, as we move like poetic prose, trying to make sense of the world. We strive to beat our opponents, to be the heroes we're meant to be.

Most of my life's stories have taken place in New England. I still drive down the same Connecticut streets I grew up near. I see ghosts of houses where shopping centers now stand as I make my way down back roads full of twists and turns where you can sneak into Massachusetts or Rhode Island without even knowing you crossed state lines. Growing up, my family had limited finances (though I never felt destitute and didn't realize we were low on funds). There were no lavish vacations. Witnessing the fireworks at the local park on the 4th of July was the summer highlight. Movies and books were my Disney World.

And yet.

I lived many adventures in the world of books. Lost in the pages of favorites: first Nursery Rhymes and Little Golden Books, then Laura Ingalls Wilder, C. S. Lewis, Judy Blume, and V. C. Andrews. Later came the classics—Dickens, F. Scott Fitzgerald, J. D. Salinger. Poetry from Dickinson, twisted tales from Poe. I even found stories in the lyrics printed inside cassette and album covers. If I didn't like the lyrics, I didn't listen to the song.

Since childhood, story surrounded me. My father often told me great adventurous stories during long walks in the woods, where he often cast me as the hero. My mother bought me countless books, which I devoured as fast as she could buy them. All the stories I heard, books I read, and movies I watched inspired me to write my own. I wrote them down in messy handwriting on torn notebook pages, recorded them on cassette tapes, and typed them on word-processors, which eventually led to desktops and laptops. I wrote on napkins and scrap pieces of paper, and yes, sometimes I even wrote poems and stories in the notes of my iPhone.

Despite all my writing, I never pondered the meaning of being a writer. The journey of authors, artists, and creatives —the world's visionaries who see beyond the colored glass— it never crossed my mind. I was just living it. I never considered what it means to write, to uncover truth and convey our experiences, sometimes in intricate detail, to tell a story. A marvelous story that, for a little while, takes the reader to a new place and time, a new journey that will somehow live in their heart and consciousness forever, changing the world, one word at a time.

I just wrote. I didn't think about the journey. Most of the time, I was just trying to survive.

Like most writers, writing was never my full time. I wrote around going to various jobs, attending college, raising children. I wrote in early mornings and late evenings, and mid afternoon lunch breaks. I wrote stories inside my head with the music turned up as I drove home from school or work in long commutes. I wondered if I'd ever publish a book. I got some stuff published. People seemed to like it. I felt scared to share it, but I did it anyway. I still remember writing the first poem I published, *Criticism of the Blood,* while tucked away in the corner of my high school library, feeling almost risqué for writing it down because how dare I write my feelings about the things I was dealing with at home in a poem with the word "blood" in the title. Was I weird? Who would read it? Was my truth offensive? Who did I think I was to send it out, hoping for publication? Imagine my delight the first time I saw my words, my heart, in black and white typeset of *The High School Writer,* a national publication that didn't have to publish my work but chose to. It inspired me. I could be a writer. I was a writer.

But what is a writer? It took me thirty more years to contemplate the thought.

One day it came to me. I was missing something about

this writer business. I was talking to another writer, joking about how I was driving my family crazy with plot ideas and wild inspirations for my current work in process. *Maybe they think I'm losing my mind,* I said. *Maybe I should stick to my day job, you know, the one that pays the bills.* And my writing friend replied—*Just tell them that's life with a writer.* I paused. What did that mean? Life with a writer? Are all writers the same? Do writers share specific experiences? Traits?

That's when the idea struck me: I was going on an adventure to find out! I knew I needed to visit as many historic writer homes as I could to find out where they lived, dreamed, hoped, and, most importantly, wrote. I wanted to feel their spaces, learn about their lives. If I could retrace their steps, maybe I could figure out what being a writer meant. Living in New England, I didn't have to travel far.

My journey to discovering what it means to be a writer was born. Soon, I'd find myself in the spaces of Twain's library, Kipling's study, Alcott's tiny desk. I found not just remnants of their history there, but myself, and you, too. All of us, right there, like living history. The human experience is one that shapes us all, through all space and time.

So, come along, join the journey with me. I'm going to take you to the homes of just a handful of some of the most remarkable historic writer homes I've visited. I'm going to show you why all of these writers are rebels.

But first, a word of caution, as lawyers like to say, the fine print.

This is not a historical documentary. Its purpose is not to be a textbook or educational work of facts. **This book is an experience, my experience, touring these homes.** Its purpose is to inspire you to reflect on your own journey. While I've read about each historic writer and have included my references in the bibliography of this book, some of my thoughts and references come from anecdotal tales shared by other guests or tour guides along the way (who knows what's true or what's folklore!) and my own thoughts and feelings during these experiences. In each chapter, I'll share these anecdotes, as well as my own reflections and discoveries. I'll provide key reflections to help inspire you along the way. I'll also share, when appropriate, which of these writers I am distantly related to according to FamilySearch.Org. Of course, it's often a very distant relationship, but fun to recognize just the same!

Overall, I encourage you to visit and experience the homes yourself. Of course, also check out the references in the back of the book and do some of your own research.

Exploring the homes of famous writers is a personal experience for the individual who visits. As I found, it can inspire you in surprising ways. I encourage you to explore their homes, museums, or even just pick up their works to learn more. Their stories are not just history, but testaments to what it means to be human.

So, what are we waiting for? Let's get right to it.

MARK TWAIN

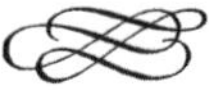

The first Mark Twain story I ever read was *A Connecticut Yankee in King Author's Court*. Time travel always gets me hooked.

Samuel Clemens, better known as Mark Twain and author of several well-known treasured stories, including: *The Adventures of Tom Sawyer, Roughing It,* and *Huckleberry Finn,* is a fascinating writer. His life, like his stories, is riddled with adventure. During his lifetime, he mined silver and gold, drove a steamboat, worked as a journalist, deserted the Confederate Militia, traveled all over the world, met Ghandi and Edison and even befriended Helen Keller and Nichola Tesla, to name just a few of his adventures.

Famous in later years for his white suit, which he unveiled in 1906 at the age of 71, when he testified about a copyright reform bill before the Congressional Joint Committee on Patents, Twain was not afraid to stand out. Reportedly, the audience "shivered" when they saw him wearing the summer clothes on a snowy December day. Twain later explained he'd reached an age where dark clothes had a "depressing effect on him."

Grief certainly wasn't far reaching from Twain's heart, having lost his father as a child, siblings, his first-born child, two daughters, and then his wife.

According to FamilySearch.Org, Mark Twain is my 8th cousin, three times removed. Here are my impressions after visiting his beloved home in Hartford, Connecticut.

* * *

MARK TWAIN'S house was the first house I visited. It was a cloudy, dreary day, and I didn't get there until sometime later in the afternoon. I instantly regretted this because I could have spent all day roaming around the grounds and inside the museum. Apart from touring the house, there were a couple of rooms near the museum gift shop that displayed photos and many of Twain's items.

Since this was the first house I visited, I had little expectation. I also came in knowing very little about Twain, aside from having read some of his stories.

THE DETAILS:

1. The house was originally built on Nook Farm, known for its park-like grounds and farmland, during a time when Hartford held over two dozen book publishers. This must have been appealing to Twain given the area's publishing opportunities and the beautiful landscape at the time.

Today, while Twain's house still stands, Nook Farm is long gone. Several apartment complexes, busy traffic, and other city bustle surround it. Twain had a very different view out his balcony during his cigar and writing breaks than the one that's there today. It's a surreal liminal space—reminding us how landscapes change. I couldn't help but wonder what Twain would think of all these changes.

. . .

2. One of the biggest surprises for me was that Harriet Beecher Stowe lived in a grey house across the lawn. Two prominent writers as neighbors! Of course, they were friends and, according to the tour guide, Harriet Beecher Stowe knew Twain's wife's family very well. This lead me to wonder . . . did Twain and Stowe discuss their current works over tea? I imagined Twain yelling to Stowe across the lawn from his balcony, *Hey Harriet, how is the writing today?* This was my first experience in learning how many historic writers either knew each other, were inspired by one another, or both.

3. Twain also had another neighbor, a lawyer, who, according to the tour guide, didn't want Twain to move in because he thought he was weird.

4. My favorite part of Twain's house was the library. It was amazing! Of course, it had shelves filled with books. There was also an intricately carved mantel, and an atrium just off the library, filled with plants. Twain would entertain his daughters here, telling them adventurous stories. According to the tour guide, his girls often played "safari" in the atrium. I learned during my visit that you can even rent this space to write! I haven't done this yet, but hope to one day.

5. Twain's actual writing space, though moved a couple times (once it was in the barn loft), was a tiny space in the corner of his billiard room. In fact, he had a larger desk in the room, but, according to the tour guide, since it faced his pool table,

it only made him think about what he'd rather be doing, other than writing. So, he had a smaller desk shoved into the corner and that's where he wrote many of his greatest works. This intrigued me the most—the man that traveled all over the world had a tiny desk in a corner to write. My writing space is tiny and so, this inspired me! In fact, you will soon learn, like I did, that many writers wrote at tiny desks.

6. Also in Twain's office/billiard room, were his pigeonhole cubbies where he kept his manuscripts. Apparently, he left *Huckleberry Finn* there for quite some time because he wasn't pleased with it. All of us writers have been there! Twain would also work on several stories at a time. When he got stuck, the manuscript went into the pigeonhole until he was ready to finish it. I liked that idea. It beats my messy desktop.

7. Twain's wife, Olivia Clemens, held his copyrights and edited all of his work. She also ran the household, oversaw staff, and homeschooled all three of their children. The room where she homeschooled them is delightful. It's a large space where I imagine many lessons took place. It was supposed to be Twain's office, but he gave it up when he realized writing next to his children's bedroom was not the best idea for a quiet setting. As a mom of two kids, I could understand.

8. The home felt filled with wonder, story, and adventure. The family did everything here: writing, playing, teaching, working. The stories the tour guide told painted a picture of a family focused home. Stories in the library, plays the children put on, exploration outside. It is said that Twain idolized his daughters, who each had a distinct personality. Susy,

it's said, was an imaginative writer. Jean, the animal activist. Clara, strong willed and the only one to outlive him. Sadly, both Susy and Jean died young. Susy died from spinal meningitis at age 24, and Jean of complications from epilepsy at 29.

9. According to the tour guide, given Twain's fiery opinions on many various topics, the family often used code words in conversations when guests came over, as a silent warning to Twain to settle down. The tour guide said that the color blue was a common code word, as his wife would say, "Don't you just love how the blue dishes match the blue vase is this room?" when he got feisty at dinner parties.

10. Twain's bed had angels on the bed posts that twisted off. His wife liked the angels looking down on her, as she often suffered headaches. The girls also loved the angels, so one is slightly lighter than the rest because they would twist the angel off the bed, using it as a bath toy.

* * *

KEY REFLECTIONS

I didn't expect to feel such a strong sense of family in Twain's house. Before my visit, I hadn't even known he had children. But as I walked through his home, I left with something deeper than just a history lesson—I left inspired.

1. Adventure Fuels Creativity

Twain's life was full of adventure. He didn't just sit at home day after day, writing. He experienced life, then he wrote about it. Often, when I am working hard on a project, I forget to take breaks or even get outside. Twain reminded me that writing requires us to live fully, not just in our imagination. While we don't need to scale mountains, we need to take breaks away from our work. We need to try new things and give ourselves the opportunity to recharge. It's in those breaks that we let our guard down, and somehow, stories find us.

2. Humor is Necessary

Twain was a master of wit, humor and satire. His humor wasn't just for laughs, though. Twain used his humor for sharp critiques of society and human nature. With humor, Twain opened readers' minds to new ways of thinking. Even the most serious stories can benefit from humor. Humor breaks tension and deepens connections. Humor is necessary in story and in life.

3. Speak Bold

Twain wasn't afraid to be bold. He said what he thought, and he stood up for what he believed in. We cannot let fear paralyze us on our writing journey. Our experiences, perspectives, and truths need to be heard, not preached, but heard. It's through story that we connect with others and their own human journeys. Impactful storytelling is authentic, not sugar-coated.

4. Perseverance

Twain faced many personal and professional challenges, including financial troubles and losing loved ones. Still, he continued to write and never gave up on his passions. His resilience resonated with me. Despite his many hardships, not only did he continue to write, but he stood up for copyright laws and inspired many other writers of his time. He reminded me that no matter what you are facing, you must show up for your art. You should never waste it.

5. Keep Wonder Alive

Twain loved telling stories to his children. Can't you just see it? Twain, sitting by the fireplace, telling loud, entertaining stories as his daughters begged for another and another. Twain never lost his sense of playfulness and curiosity. It's important to face every day with wonder, finding the magic in each moment.

CONCLUSION: LIFE IS AN ADVENTURE

As I stood on Twain's porch, I couldn't help but ask myself: How can I live my life as an adventure? Twain's legacy isn't just in the books he wrote, but in the life he lived. I wondered, what about other writers? If I could be so inspired by one afternoon of walking through the empty rooms where Twain once lived, what else would I find on my journey?

LOUISA MAY ALCOTT

Louisa May Alcott, most widely known for being the author of *Little Women,* wrote over 30 novels, short story collections and poems, including *Little Men,* and *Jo's Boys.*

Daughter of noted transcendentalist Amos Bronson Alcott and Abigail May III, Louisa May grew up in Boston and Concord, Massachusetts. My visit took place at the Orchard House in Concord, where Alcott most famously wrote *Little Women.* I'd always admired her stories and couldn't wait to see where she dreamed, lived and wrote. The following are my impressions from the visit and tidbits of information learned from the tour.

* * *

IT WAS a gorgeous early spring day when I visited Alcott's home. The daffodils were in full bloom, and the warm spring air felt welcoming after a long, cold winter. It sounds naïve, but I had no idea what I was in for going to Concord. So many writers and adventures around every corner. Ralph

Waldo Emerson! Henry David Thoreau! Nathanial Hawthorne! Margaret Sidney! Just to name a few. But those would be adventures for other days (and other volumes of *Rebel Writers*). For me, the Concord journey began with Louisa May Alcott.

THE DETAILS

1. The Orchard House is a lovely Colonial, set amongst the New England Woods, making it easy to envision her life at this time (as compared to my experience at Mark Twain's house, which is now nestled in the city).

2. Louisa May wrote for long hours at a time. Sometimes—14 hours! Remember, she didn't have a typewriter, so she was handwriting all that time. She taught herself to write with both hands to prevent cramping.

3. The family had a "mood pillow" on the couch that when turned straight up was a warning to others that Louisa May was in a "mood." I guess she got cranky from writing so long?

4. I loved standing in the dining room where she and her sisters put on many plays. Upstairs, they still have the trunk with some of the girls' former costumes and props. You could almost feel her love of story standing in these rooms.

5. Her father was a vigorous proponent of transcendentalism. A pioneer educator, he believed in empowering others, was the inventor of school recess, and

encouraged his girls to be educated. His reputation, however, suffered for his beliefs, affecting his work prospects. Ralph Waldo Emerson often supported the Alcott family bills when money was tight. Alcott herself also supported her family with money made from her novels. In fact, she wrote *Jo's Boys* to help with her sister's finances.

6. Alcott had quite the neighbors and friends. Ralph Waldo Emerson, who often let her borrow books, lived just down the street, as well as Henry David Thoreau. Nathaniel Hawthorne also bought her childhood home, where many of the events of *Little Women* occurred. So many writers on one street! Together in life and the afterlife, each of these writers' last resting places is in the same row at Sleepy Hollow Cemetery—at "Author's Ridge." I visited Author's Ridge on the same day, where I found pens and pencils left on the graves of each of these prominent writers.

7. Louisa May Alcott wasn't just a writer. She was also a nurse in the Civil War. Thus, while *Little Women* was autobiographical, in reality, it was Alcott that went to war, not her father.

8. Another difference between the novel and real life is that the girls were much older in the era she wrote them in. Her sister Elizabeth, the only sister whose true name appears in the novel, died at age 18, ten years before.

9. She wrote *Little Women* in under three months! Those 14-hour workdays paid off. Alcott had a passion for writing

from a young age, starting with poetry. In her lifetime, she studied under Ralph Waldo Emerson, Henry David Thoreau, and Nathaniel Hawthorne.

10. Her desk was small and made by her father. It was a tiny board built into the wall, facing two windows. Like Twain, her desk was small. It was, in fact, much smaller than Twain's, proving that you don't need an elaborate space to write great stories.

KEY REFLECTIONS

1. Secrets of Tenacity

Louisa May Alcott had tenacity. How else do you explain 14-hour writing jaunts? Writing also wasn't Alcott's only job, as she undertook several to help support her family. During her lifetime, she was a teacher, a governess, a seamstress, and a nurse. Although her early works met with little success, she continued to write despite her many challenges. Her powerful will and tenacity reminded me that success is not immediate. It takes a steady determination and faith in ourselves to overcome adversity. When I think of Alcott, I think of the girl switching from her left hand to her right, up long hours to write the stories of her heart. Those stories continue to inspire readers today.

2. Lead a Fulfilling Life

Alcott was fiercely independent. While Alcott herself never married or had children, when her sister died, she adopted her niece. Alcott was a nurse during the Civil War, where she comforted dying soldiers and assisted doctors performing amputations. She advocated to abolish slavery, but typhoid fever cut short her efforts when it made her ill. Alcott was also a huge advocate for women's rights. In fact, Alcott was the first woman to register to vote in Concord, Massachusetts.

She lived a rich life, staying true to her own values and path as both a writer and woman of the 19th century. Alcott reminded me of the value of standing firm in our beliefs and to remember to trust ourselves. To live a fulfilling life, we need to use our talents not just for personal gain, but to uplift and support others along the way.

3. The Power of Your Own Story

Alcott didn't initially want to write *Little Women.* It wasn't her style. She'd been writing more racy Gothic thrillers under a pen name A.M. Barnard to earn money prior to writing *Little Women.* When asked by a publisher in 1868 to write a girls' story, she noted in her diary that she "never liked girls or knew many, except my sisters." Mostly, however, I think Alcott didn't think a simple tale about a group of sisters would interest readers, especially since her tale would reflect so much of her own life growing up in a modest family.

Despite her reluctance, Alcott took on the challenge, creating the heartfelt story we still treasure today.

Sometimes, we think our stories aren't important. That, like adventures, they need to be grand and spectacular. But the spectacular lies in everyday life. The moments that build our character give voice to our souls. It's through these stories we build connections with others that will continue to inspire generations to come because we recognize ourselves, as history progresses, in those simple stories of everyday life no matter the era. So, believe in your story. You never know how it might resonate.

. . .

CONCLUSION: FIGHT FOR YOUR DREAMS

Louisa May Alcott's life had a profound impact on me, leaving me both impressed and inspired. She suffered immense poverty and heartache, but still came out strong, never giving up on her dreams. In a time when women were marginalized, she took care of her family and surrounded herself with some of history's finest writers and thinkers.

There are so many lessons to be had from Alcott's life. Alcott reminds us to stand up for what we believe in and to never stop fighting for our dreams. As I stepped away from Alcott's home, I realized that writing is not just a solitary act. Alcott's friendships with other writers, especially Emerson and Thoreau, were instrumental in her growth as a writer. Love of story can bring people, not just writers, together in inspiring ways. Writing is difficult and having trusted peers who share your love for storytelling is essential for pushing your skills to reach new heights.

So where did my journey take me next? To the streets of Salem and ghosts of Nathanial Hawthorne, of course!

NATHANIAL HAWTHORNE

I learned about Nathaniel Hawthorne in high school, when I read *The Scarlet Letter*. I knew right then and there he was one of my favorite historic writers. What I didn't know at the time is that Hawthorne (at least according to Familysearch.com) is my 7th cousin, four times removed on the maternal side of my family. We share the same 10th great grandparents: John Woodbury and Agnes Napper circa mid 1500s to early 1600s.

Hawthorne, as I found with other writers, such as Robert Frost, is a journey to discover. There isn't one place to visit to learn about his life. You can visit his home, The Wayside, in Concord, Mass, which Hawthorne bought from Louisa May Alcottt's family in 1852. The Wayside is the actual location where the events described in Alcott's *Little Women* took place. It was also later home to children's author, Harriet Lothrop (pen name Margaret Sidney), who wrote F*ive Little Peppers*.

I also found that throughout my journey to various homes, Hawthorne seemed to show up. Poet Emily Dickinson admired his work, he knew Emerson, Thoreau, and Alcott. He was close friends with Herman Melville. I'll talk more about Melville later on in this book, and the rest of the writers Hawthorne is connected to in Volume 2 when it releases. But for now, this journey with Hawthorne for me started in Salem, Massachusetts, at the House of the Seven Gables.

* * *

I VISITED the House of the Seven Gables in June, which, to be honest, at the time felt sort of off visiting Salem this time of year. As a New Englander, I've always headed to Salem during Halloween because, well, witches, of course. I'd soon find, however, that there is so much more history to this historic New England town than one tiny snapshot of history. Some of that history includes the life of Nathaniel Hawthorne.

THE DETAILS—ON HAWTHORNE

1. Nathanial Hawthorne was born in Salem, Mass on July 4, 1804, to Elizabeth Manning and Captain Nathanial Hawthorne in a circa-1750 home. The home he was born in is located at the House of the Seven Gables museum as an additional self-guided tour. It was relocated to the grounds of the museum by the non-profit House of the Seven Gables Settlement Association.

His birth home was actually built a few blocks away on Union Street around 1750, and later moved to the museum's campus in 1958. It was Hawthorne's cousin, Susanna Ingersoll, who lived at the House of the Seven Gables. Hawthorne would often visit her at the house, inspiring him to write the book, which fun fact, I learned when visiting Herman Melville's house that Hawthorne was working on writing *The House of the Seven Gables* when he became friends with the Moby Dick author. Between the House of the Seven Gables and Hawthorne's birth home, both being on location at the museum makes it one of the most important Hawthorne sites in the world.

2. Hawthorne's birth family was long associated with the town of Salem. In fact, Hawthorne's great-great-grandfather, John Hathorne, was the judge who oversaw the Salem Witch Trials. Nathanial originally spelled his last name as "Hathorne" but changed it in college by adding the "w." It's speculated he wanted to distance himself from his painful ancestry. I can't blame him—I was relieved when I looked at my ancestry and confirmed that while Hawthorne is my distant cousin, I am not blood related to the Salem Judge.

3. Hawthorne's father died while at sea with yellow fever when Hawthorne was just four years old. It was heart-breaking to hear that he lost his father so young. Likely, this affected in him many ways.

4. As a child, he spent most of his time growing up in Salem, as well as in Maine, near Sebago Lake. He loved Sebago Lake. I can't say I disagree. Sebago Lake has always been one of my favorite places. Nestled amid tall pines reaching to the sky, it's a lovely serene place that's worth a visit.

. . .

5. Around the age of nine, Hawthorne was bedridden for a year after being hit on the leg playing "bat and ball." Apparently, he became lame, during which time several physicians could find nothing wrong with him.

6. In his teens, he wrote a private newspaper for his family called "The Spectator" for fun. The homemade publication was written by hand and included poems, humor, essays and stories. I loved this so much. It reminded me of the many construction paper books I created as a child, as well as all the plays and "concerts" I put on for my family when I was a kid. It reminded me that when you are an artist, you burst with creative energy, especially as a child. I imagined Hawthorne was bursting with his own creative energy, inspiring him to write the private newspaper in his spare time.

7. Hawthorne studied at Bowdoin College, beginning in 1821. It was there that he met future president, Franklin Pierce and future poet, Henry Wadsworth Longfellow. This was especially interesting to me because President Pierce is my 4th cousin 6x removed—from my maternal great grandfather's bloodline (Hawthorne is from my maternal great grandmother's bloodline). It seems New England is full of historic connections.

8. Hawthorne was a family man. He married Sophia Peabody, who was known to have been reclusive, like Hawthorne. The two had three children: Una, Julian and Rose. Family was important to Hawthorne. I think this quote from one of Hawthorne's letters to Bowdoin class-

mate, Horatio Bridge, sums up Hawthorne's view of family best:

> "Every true & happy family is a soul-system that outshines all the solar-systems in space & time."

9. Rose Hawthorne, Nathaniel's daughter, initially pursued a literary career like her father. She converted to Roman Catholicism with her husband, and then, after the death of her child and husband, she moved into a tenement in an impoverished New York City neighborhood where she nursed cancer patients. She then became nun, Mother Mary Alphonsa. In 2003, she was nominated for sainthood.

10. By Presidential appointment, Hawthorne served as the Port of Salem's Surveyor from 1846 to 1849 at The Custom House. It was here that Hawthorne came up with the idea for *The Scarlet Letter*. People say that he spent so much time pacing and meditating on this story in between work that his pacing wore out the floor at The Custom House. On the day I visited, The Custom House was closed, however, I had been there before many years ago where I saw Nathanial Hawthorne's desk.

11. According to one of the tour guides at Hawthorne's birth home, Hawthorne did not feel thrilled to be back in Salem during his years working at The Custom House. He was not a fan of his childhood town and wanted to separate from its painful history. When Hawthorne was working at The Custom House, it was a busy port. I imagined Hawthorne must have spent some time on his breaks staring out at the water.

. . .

THE DETAILS—ON THE HOUSE OF THE SEVEN GABLES

1. As mentioned earlier, Hawthorne himself never lived at the House of the Seven Gables, which belonged to his cousin Susannah. While visiting, Susannah often shared talks of the home's history with Hawthorne over long talks.

2. The House of Seven Gables is a marvel in itself, rich in history in its design. It even has a secret staircase!

Word of caution: if you are claustrophobic, avoid taking it. It was too narrow for me, so I took another back staircase (that was much wider) with the tour guide.

3. Philanthropist and preservationist Caroline Emmerton turned into a museum, The House of Seven Gables. You can find out more about the history of the museum's founding at its website, noted in the bibliography.

4. The first official "gift shop" of Salem was at The House of the Seven Gables. It was inside a cubby in the wall that happened up to display various trinkets for guests to buy.

5. There's a wonderful space in the house's attic, where the tour guide gives you a glimpse with a 3d model on how the house came to be "The House of the Seven Gables." The attic

has been largely unchanged. Even though it's been said that Hawthorne and his cousin Susannah spent much of their time in the parlor space downstairs (where the wallpaper is hand painted!), I liked to imagine them hanging out in the home's attic, swapping stories. Another fascinating fact about the house? In 1940, a film adaptation of the story *The House of the Seven Gables* was made.

KEY REFLECTIONS

1. WRITERS HAVE TO PAY THE BILLS

It's a fact many writers and artist (like all of us) must face: paying the bills. Like many writers, Hawthorne had to work other jobs to make ends meet. His permanent path where he paced at The Custom House reminds us that even when working other jobs, writers can't escape their stories. While I'm sure Hawthorne was grateful for his various jobs (he had a family to support), I'm sure he was most inspired when writing his stories. Hawthorne teaches us that sometimes we do what we have to do, but we must still fight for our right to write, or do whatever it is that sets our hearts ablaze. If your heart burns with passion for your story, you'll carve out the time. Even if it means squeezing in writing during your lunch break (or in Hawthorne's case, during his downtime at The Custom House).

2. TRAUMA CAN IMPACT GENERATIONS

Hawthorne was inspired by history and intrigued by how trauma can affect individuals and families for years to come. He was especially interested in writing about hypocrisy. His works often explore history, emphasizing how the past can have lingering effects on the present. In stories like *The House of the Seven Gables,* Hawthorne explored the idea that past sins can haunt future generations. It's important as writers to explore history, both our personal and collective histories, because it deepens our connections and the emotional resonance of our stories. By looking at our histories, we can dig deeper into the complexities of characters and motivations, perhaps even by telling cautious tales to help us learn from the past.

3. WRITING IS SELF-DISCOVERY

Hawthorne used writing to explore his own inner thoughts, beliefs, and moral questions. Through his stories, he delved into themes of guilt, sin, and redemption, further exploring his own fears and curiosities. The act of storytelling requires self-reflection. It is the opportunity to uncover truths of society, but most importantly, our own inner truths. Writing deepens our understanding of our lives and the human experience by allowing us to process emotions, question beliefs, and discover who we are.

4. KEEP GOING

Despite Hawthorne's moderate success of *The Scarlet Letter* (1850) and *The House of the Seven Gables* (1851), he could never solely live on an income of writing fiction. He continued to work over the years as an editor, surveyor, inspector, and even as a United States consul in Liverpool. There were times he struggled to write. It's said that in April 1846, after being official appointed the Surveyor of the District of Salem and Beverly and Inspector of the Revenue for the Port of Salem, he admitted to author Henry Wadsworth Longfellow:

> "I am trying to resume my pen ... Whenever I sit alone, or walk alone, I find myself dreaming about stories, as of old; but these forenoons in the Custom House undo all that the afternoons and evenings have done. I should be happier if I could write."

Despite Hawthorne's financial and personal struggles, Hawthorne stayed true to developing stories by both living them and writing them.

5. STAY TRUE TO YOUR VOICE

Hawthorne stayed true to his artistic vision, often resisting to conform to the literary trends of his time and writing instead on the things that obsessed him: exploring the human condition, sin, guilt, and redemption. He wasn't afraid to explore these darker trends, despite the criticism he faced for it. The impact of *The Scarlet Letter,* for example, is a testament to how powerful staying true to one's artistic vision is. To this day, *The Scarlet Letter* is read in schools, referenced in popular story, mentioned in song lyrics. His life shows not just a passion for uncovering what it means to be human, but illustrates the importance of artistic integrity. Rather than changing his style to "fit the trends," he wrote stories that were meaningful to him. A storyteller's deepest impact on the world is when they tell the story that only they can tell. That takes courage and staying true to your voice.

CONCLUSION: ALWAYS BE YOU

Hawthorne fascinates me, not just because of his commitment to his voice and story, but how he navigated life in a unique time of American history. Hawthorne teaches us to never give up on being who we are by staying true to our voice, our craft, our talents, no matter what the world tells us we should be or do. Only you can tell your story. No one needs another version of somebody else. The world needs you.

H.P. LOVECRAFT

Howard Phillips Lovecraft, better known as H. P. Lovecraft, was an American writer of the "weird and strange" science, fantasy, and horror fiction. Best known for his creation of the Cthulhu Mythos, Lovecraft spent most of his life in New England, primarily, Providence.

Private owners reside at all of Lovecraft's homes (and some were relocated to accommodate some of Brown University's buildings). Therefore, to visit Lovecraft sites, you need to go on a "secret journey." I'm calling it "secret" because for those who know, they know. But I'll let you in on the secret!

To see the life of Lovecraft, you need to take *The Lovecraft's College Hill Walking Tour*. You can get a map at the *Lovecraft Arts and Science Bookstore* in Providence at *The Arcade,* which, fun fact, is in the first enclosed shopping mall in America.

But back to the journey. So, you go to this bookstore inside *The Arcade* and ask for the map. Be sure to checkout all the books there too. If you are a fantasy, horror and/or science fiction fan, this place is for you. I found so many interesting books and items in this store that I've never seen anywhere else, including a replica of H.P. Lovecraft's own writing journal (though I did later find it is available online as well).

Once you get the map, you will see that it lists all the various locations where H.P. lived, dreamed, and wrote. I have to be honest, I felt a bit intimidated by the map at first. I've never been good at directions. Still, I set out on the journey to discover Lovecraft, quickly finding a lifetime in a handful of streets in Providence.

Word of caution: most of the tour is uphill, so bring your walking shoes! Also another tip: you might find the map online through searching just in case you can't get to the store.

* * *

THE DAY I ventured throughout Providence was a damp, dark day. Thankfully, the rain held off for most of my tour. Still, the grey ambiance certainly added to the spooky ambiance of discovering the life of the horror science fiction writer.

THE DETAILS

1. H. P. Lovecraft was born at 9 a.m. on August 20, 1890, at his family home at what is now 454 Angell Street in Providence, Rhode Island. Lovecraft could trace his ancestry on his mother's side back to 1630. His father, a traveling salesperson for Gorham & Co., Silversmiths, of Providence, suffered a nervous breakdown in a hotel room in Chicago when Lovecraft was just three years old. Lovecraft's father then entered an institution, where he remained for five years before passing away on July 19, 1898.

. . .

2. The death of his father left Lovecraft and his mother to live with his grandfather. Thankfully, his grandfather was quite wealthy, giving Lovecraft some opportunity. However, after his grandfather died, the wealth dissipated. Lovecraft lived with his mother as funds ran dry. However, his mother eventually experienced a nervous breakdown and was institutionalized in 1919. She then died in 1921 after a gall bladder operation. This devastated Lovecraft.

3. During his youth, Lovecraft was close to his two aunts, however, his grandfather was the most influential. His grandfather, Whipple Van Buern Phillips, was a prominent industrialist. It's said that Lovecraft himself was reciting poetry at age two, reading at age three, and writing by six or seven. His earliest enthusiasm for books was for the *Arabian Nights*. He also loved Greek mythology. His grandfather, who often entertained Lovecraft with weird gothic tales, fostered his interest in the weird.

4. Lovecraft suffered from frequent illnesses as a boy. People believed that most of his illnesses were psychological. I can't help but wonder if it wasn't from all the stress he was facing, given his various family issues. He attended school sporadically, but learned mostly through independent reading. He ended up attending Hope Street High School, where both his teachers and peers encouraged his writing.

5. Lovecraft's first appearance in print was in 1906, when he wrote a letter on an astronomical matter to The Providence Sunday Journal. In fact, he wrote a monthly astronomy column for *The Pawtuxet Valley Gleaner,* a rural paper and

later wrote columns for *The Providence Tribune* (1906–08) and *The Providence Evening News* (1914–18), as well as *The Asheville (N.C.) Gazette-News* (1915).

6. Lovecraft liked to bike ride until around 1908 when he because severely ill. After that, he only rode until 1913, when he gave it up. There are several quotes from Lovecraft about riding his bicycle. My favorite is this one from 1904:

> "The late Prof. Upton of Brown, a friend of the family, gave me the freedom of the college observatory, (Ladd Observatory) & I came & went there at will on my bicycle." The "Ladd Observatory tops a considerable eminence about a mile from the house."

Lovecraft wheeled the bicycle up and rode it down the hill on the quick trip home. While on my walk, I stood on the steps of the *Ladd Observatory*, where Lovecraft spent so much time as a child. I stared down the street he once rode his bike wildly down, imagining the joy he must have felt in those fleeting moments, alive on his bicycle. So much of his life was tragic, so being in that space where we know he came to dream gave a glimpse into the moments he felt happy and free. I felt so inspired, I wrote a poem, which I will include at the end of this chapter.

7. Lovecraft was supposed to graduate high school in 1908, however, he suffered from another unidentified health crisis, which was more severe than his prior illnesses. To this day, the exact circumstances are unknown. Some records point to Lovecraft's own correspondence in which he describes it as a "nervous collapse" and "sort of breakdown." He blames it in

these letters on the stress of high school, even though he enjoyed school. He still maintained he was going to attend Brown University, however, he never graduated and never attended school again. It's heartbreaking to imagine Lovecraft never setting foot in the college he yearned for, even though it was practically in his own backyard. In Lovecraft's words, in a letter stating the events of 1908, he stated,

> "I was and am prey to intense headaches, insomnia, and general nervous weakness which prevents my continuous application to anything."

8. Part of the walking tour includes a visit to The Providence Atheneum. Built in 1838, the famous Edgar Allan Poe (who, according to FamilySearch.Org is my 8th cousin, 4x removed) also visited this library once upon a time. Lovecraft himself spent hours here, writing and revising, more than a half a century after Poe. I highly recommend visiting here. It's older than the Library of Congress, and besides Poe and Lovecraft, other famous visitors came here, including Sarah Whitman, whom Poe had a passionate and tumultuous relationship with.

9. As talented as Lovecraft was, and as tragic as his life came to be, we can't talk about Lovecraft without mentioning that in recent decades, the view that Lovecraft was a racist has become a well-known topic for discussion. Some scholars argue that Lovecraft's own letters are filled with racist views and that these prejudices are reflected in some of his stories. While his literary contributions to horror and weird fiction are significant, it's important to acknowledge that racism is not acceptable, forcing us to confront these harmful aspects of his legacy. Perhaps understanding the context of the age in

which he lived and the surroundings of his childhood can allow us to critically engage with his work while condemning the bigotry he expressed. This was an aspect I didn't know when I started the journey exploring Lovecraft, and honestly, broke my heart to know.

10. Lovecraft married Sonia Greene, and for a short time, lived in NYC. For a short time, things went well. Lovecraft became part of the Kalem Club, which was an informal group of literary and intellectual friends who encouraged him to submit to *Weird Tales*. Several of his works were published in *Weird Tales,* including "Under the Pyramids" which was ghostwritten for Harry Houdini.

When Sonia had to move for work, however, things went downhill. Lovecraft stayed in NYC but became lonely. Soon after, Sonia lost her business and assets in a bank failure. Lovecraft tried to support her, but his lack of experience in jobs was an issue. Lovecraft had the opportunity to become the editor of *Weird Tales,* but he turned it down, stating he did not want to move to Chicago. Sonia then became ill, moved to Cincinnati, and traveled for work. She sent Lovecraft a weekly allowance to help support his tiny apartment. After losing approximately 40 pounds, he then went back to Providence in 1933 to live with his aunts, which would be his last home.

Lovecraft died in 1937 with cancer of the small intestine. You can visit Lovecraft's grave, but if you do, I recommend doing some research to find it at the Swan Point Cemetery in Providence. It's a bit hidden and hard to find if you don't know where you are going.

KEY REFLECTIONS

1. STAY WEIRD

Lovecraft's life was filled with periods of tragedy and isolation. Still, he didn't let it stifle him. Instead, he channelled his inner struggles into stories that faced his deep-seated fears head on. Don't be afraid to be weird and don't be afraid to use story to work through your fears.

2. GROW PAST YOUR FLAWS

Lovecraft's views on race and culture were undeniably problematic. Still, we can use it as a cautionary tale by reflecting on its life. As creators, we must recognize our own biases and continually challenge them as we evolve as artists and human beings. Acknowledging our flaws can only open the door to growth and for impactful, meaningful stories that help shape us into being better, more empathetic, and inclusive human beings.

3. SOMETIMES, WE DON'T SEE OUR SUCCESS

Lovecraft didn't see his success during his lifetime, but that didn't make his work any less important. His work went on to inspire generations of writers, filmmakers, and artists. His life is a powerful reminder that creative success does not come immediately. The impact of your work may be long after you're done. Keep creating anyway. You never know who or how you might inspire others when they need it the most.

CONCLUSION: TELL YOUR STORY, NO MATTER HOW WEIRD

The experience of visiting Lovecraft's life in Providence

left me feeling more melancholic rather than inspired. I felt sadness for the little boy who experienced the loss of his dad and his grandfather, suffered from illnesses, and later had to face the institutionalization of his mother. Learning about some of the views he held also disheartened me.

Still, I recognized that despite his pain, he kept on writing weird, strange tales that many still read and reflect on today. Lovecraft therefore teaches us that no matter what, you should always tell your story, no matter how weird, because through stories, we learn and grow to be better human beings.

Lovecraft's Providence - A Poem

By: Sarah Crowne

In distant spaces
Time lapsed.
Iron gates and street lanterns,
Now gone dark -
In vacant lands
Of earth
Where landscapes shift,
But skylines, sometimes,
Remain the same.

Here, on these steps of the observatory -
A young boy dreamt stories far and wide.
Fantastical
Inklings of his heart
Yet to be told to the world.

Now, standing on these steps,
Separated only by time and space -
I stare at the door,
Understanding, for the first time,
How the curiosities of life
Entangle us -
And also set us free.

GERTRUDE CHANDLER WARNER

It was a sweet surprise to discover Gertrude Chandler Warner. The famous schoolteacher/author who introduced us to the fabulous *The Boxcar Children's Series* was nothing short of remarkable. Want to hear the best part? She was in my backyard, living just a hop and a skip away from my hometown.

Warner's home is privately owned; therefore, I couldn't visit it. I did get the opportunity, however, to visit the *Gertrude Chandler Warner The Boxcar Children Museum* in Putnam, CT, which is, you guessed it, a vintage boxcar.

Born on April 16, 1890, Warner lived until 1979 in the town of Putnam. In fact, Warner lived, worked, and was ultimately buried in places just a few short square miles of one another, reiterating the point that one can have whole adventures without traveling far.

* * *

I've lived close to Putnam my entire life and, as such, have passed the museum at least a hundred times. I still can't believe it took me so long to visit the museum. It was an early spring day when I visited, and quite busy at the museum that day. What struck me most about my visit were the many parallels Warner and I shared in our life stories. The train tracks she used to gaze out at as a child, dreaming of living in a boxcar, are the same trains tracks I used to walk as a little girl with my dad. Like Warner, I was also a schoolteacher, and once taught in the same district she taught in. I took an oath to become an attorney and worked in the same court her father had served as a judge.

The Gertrude Chandler Warner The Boxcar Children Museum is filled with wonder and is highly recommended for a visit. Here are the fun facts I learned while visiting.

THE DETAILS

1. Upon my visit, a man who was once a student in Ms. Warner's class greeted me! He was a wealth of information and so passionate about his former teacher and favorite writer. Not only was he a former student, but he was also a character in her books. In fact, he told me that many of her students made their way into her stories. He confirmed that she always asked permission to include them, and the kids were excited to be in her books.

2. The school building Warner used to teach at is no longer a school, but an apartment building. I've always known the building as the "School Street Apartments" and never stopped to think about the fact it was, once upon a time, a school. It wasn't just any school, though, it was the school where one of America's most beloved teachers and talented authors once taught.

. . .

3. Back in the day, Warner let her students play musical instruments as loud as possible during the school day as they had their own "marching band." I guess maybe that wasn't popular amongst the other teachers, but I'm sure the kids loved it (and as a former teacher that put the kids' hands-on experiences over scripted book work first, I can relate to her passion!) Warner herself played the cello.

4. Because of frequent illnesses, Warner never finished high school. She was called to teach during WW1, when there was a shortage of teachers because of many male teachers being called to serve in the war. Warner taught first grade. For a short time, she taught third grade. Thus, some students were fortunate to have this well-loved teacher twice. Warner was a teacher in Putnam from 1918 to 1950.

5. During the summer months, Warner returned to school for education courses at Yale University. Yale University was so impressed with her teaching methods, they suggested that she teach there.

6. Warner's favorite childhood book was *Alice's Adventures in Wonderland.* Warner knew her calling as an author at just five years old. Since a child, she filled her notebooks with her stories. If you visit the museum, you can see some of her notebooks from her time writing as an adult.

7. Warner's first book, *The House of Delight,* was published by The Pilgrim Press and sold 1,000 copies. *The Boxcar Children* was first published by Rand McNally Co. in 1924. Warner

dreamed up *The Boxcar Children* while sick at home with bronchitis. She claimed she wrote it because she always dreamed what it would be like to live in a boxcar.

8. *The Emblem Club* chose her as "Woman of the Year" in 1965 for her dedicated work toward education and the American Red Cross.

9. When *The Boxcar Children* was first published, many librarians disapproved of the book. They complained the children were having too much fun without the parents telling them what to do. Of course, this is why so many kids loved it!

10. Warner's final resting place is at the Grove Street Cemetery in Putnam. No pens or pencils, unlike Authors Row at Sleepy Hollow. But her gravestone holds a most beautiful quote.

> "She opens her mouth with wisdom and the teaching of kindness is on her tongue."

KEY REFLECTIONS

1. Childhood Dreams Can Come True: Warner knew from a young age she wanted to be a writer. It's inspiring that she grew up to be one. So many times, we dream things as children and never fulfill those hopes. Or if we do, we don't fulfill all of them because we think we can only be one thing. There is nothing further from the truth. I believe as children we know our genuine passions, and often move away from them because of life's responsibilities. However, it's never too late and you don't have to be one thing. You can always make time for your passions, even if you have to fight for it.

2. You Can Face Health Challenges: Warner faced many health challenges throughout her life. Despite this, she turned these challenges into opportunity as she used the time to focus on her writing. Her perseverance in the face of adversity lead to creating *The Boxcar Children Series,* which has been beloved by generations of readers. Warner reminds us that no matter what you are going through, you must always push forward, striving to make your dreams come true.

3. You Can Have More Than One Passion: Warner wasn't just a writer; she was a schoolteacher. It was apparent at the museum, reading the various quotes from former students, meeting a former student, and seeing the various displays of her past curriculums, that she wasn't just a schoolteacher, either. She was a *beloved* schoolteacher. As a former teacher myself, I know that you can't be a beloved teacher unless you truly care about your students and class. Warner went beyond her responsibilities to make every child feel special, whether it was through organizing marching bands or planning special birthday surprises for her students. This proves that you can, in fact, have more than one passion. Warner's passions encompassed teaching, writing, community involvement, and stargazing. She lived a rich life in a small town, leaving a legacy behind.

. . .

Conclusion: When You Put Your Passions First, You Can Accomplish Anything.

What are you waiting for? You can love and be many things. You can accomplish anything you set your mind to. As I continued on my journey, I found this lesson repeatedly, as so many writers faced significant challenges ranging from health, grief, finances, etc. But they kept on writing. Just like you can continue to evolve to be *your* true self.

RUDYARD KIPLING

Did you know Rudyard Kipling wrote *The Jungle Book* while living in the snowy mountains of Vermont?

Kipling's Naulakha, in Dummerston, Vermont, is just down the street from Brattleboro. Owned by *The Landmark Trust,* this home is only available for daily visitor tours once a year for the *Rhododendron Tour*. If you can't make the yearly tour, this house is also available to rent for your next writer's retreat, where you can sit and write at Kipling's desk. Imagine, writing where Kipling penned favorites such as *The Jungle Book, Captains Courageous* and portions of the *Just So Stories*!

This tour was one of my favorites. The house, nestled on top of a hill overlooking Vermont, is unique because it resembles a ship. Kipling himself expressed his desire for the home to resemble a ship "sailing across the Vermont countryside."

* * *

I VISITED this house in early June, during the Rhododendron tour. The flowers were in full bloom and were absolutely gorgeous. The Rhododendrons create a tunnel like path which you can walk through. It was stunning, to say the least.

THE DETAILS

1. Rudyard Kipling was born in Bombay, India on December 30, 1965. However, he spent much of his life in England. He died on January 18, 1936, in London. Kipling wrote short stories, novels and poetry. In 1907, Rudyard Kipling received the Nobel Prize for Literature.

2. Reports indicate that much of Kipling's childhood was unhappy. His parents left him at a foster home in Southsea at six years old, where he lived for five years. He described much of these horrors in the story, "Baa Baa, Black Sheep" (1888).

3. As Kipling grew older, he returned to India in 1882, where he worked for seven years as a journalist. It was during this time that much of his first writings, including several short stories, were published in various journals.

4. Kipling married his American-born wife, Caroline, in 1892. Caroline was the sister of Wolcott Balestier, who was an American publisher and writer. They moved with their daughter, Josephine, into Naulakha in the summer of 1893 and remained there for three full years.

. . .

5. THE NAME, "NAULAKHA" is Hindi for "priceless jewel." The house is three stories, plus a basement. The tour allowed you to explore everywhere, even the basement, on your own terms. There's something cool about exploring every inch of a historic writer's home, from the ancient water heater in the depths of his basement to the billiard room on the top floor. Even the tub is original. Fun fact: Kipling's billiard room was inspired by Mark Twain's. Kipling had seen it on a visit and built his own similar room when he moved to Vermont.

6. The years at Naulakha were productive for Kipling, as he wrote from 9 to 12 each day. As a visitor, you can explore his study and sit at his desk. Large windows overlook the Vermont landscape, and a giant wall of bookshelves made me want to kick back and spend the day reading all afternoon. Of course, you couldn't touch the books, but just being near the collection that inspired Kipling was enough for me!

7. Kipling described Naulakha as "[n]inety feet was the length of it and thirty the width, on a high foundation of solid mortared rocks which gave us an airy and a skunk-proof basement. The rest was wood, shingled, roof and sides, with dull green hand-split shingles, and the windows were lavish and wide." It's a spectacular home, with incredible staircases that bring you to all levels. There are plenty of windows and balconies to stand and look out at the landscape from as well. No wonder he found it so inspiring.

8. His wife, Caroline, kept a diary that ran *13,000 pages!* On the 31st of December each year, she'd ask her husband to pen a remark that summed up the prior 12 months. On

December 31, 1894, he wrote, "Carrie tots up the books and finds that I have this year earned $25,000 . . . Not that mine be the praise; Carrie deserves it all." He was a man that appreciated his wife!

9. Kipling left Vermont after a court case with his brother-in-law. There seem to be several versions of this story pieced together by different writers. Kipling himself, however, does not even mention the hearing or his brother-in-law in his autobiography or his letters. Since Kipling didn't focus on it, neither will we, however, if you want to 'spill the tea' it seems his brother-in-law's failure to account for showing the larger sums of money he had spent on Naulakha was the main reason for the dispute.

10. At one point, so many fans started showing up to see Kipling's house that onlookers who would pay to stare across the road hoping to see Kipling out on his deck built a tower across the street. Kipling was not a fan. Fans were lining up to spy on him. While I am sure he appreciated reader support, he needed privacy to live and write, after all.

It wasn't long after that Kipling left Vermont.

KEY REFLECTIONS

1. YOU CAN OVERCOME YOUR PAST.

Kipling faced childhood trauma after spending time in a foster home where he and his sister faced abuse. Kipling became a Nobel Prize Author, proving that you should never let your past define you. I find it inspiring that despite his unhappy childhood, he wrote such wonderful stories, such as *The Jungle Book,* for children, bringing entertainment and fun to children of all ages for generations to come.

2. FAMILY DRAMA SHOULDN'T STOP YOU

Kipling didn't let his grievance with his brother-in-law get him down. While I am sure the drama was not something that excited him, he didn't play into it and refused to write about it in his biography. Whether he was hiding from it or didn't want to be engaged with it, or both, I admire his ability to stand tall, move forward, and not let it get him down. There's always going to be some kind of drama in our lives, but we can't let that stop us from living the best life we can live.

3. WRITE THROUGH YOUR GRIEF

Sadly, Kipling's young daughter Josephine died at age 6 from pneumonia. His only son, John Kipling, died in action in WW1 at 18. Thus, Kipling was no stranger to grief. Yet still, he persevered on, using themes of remembrance, loss, and the fleeting nature of life in his later stories and poems. Kipling reminds us that writing can be healing, as we dare to put our pens to paper, writing the things that plague us the most. He found strength in his writing, even after the unimaginable loss of his children. These experiences changed his personal beliefs about the world. It was through writing that he could make sense of it.

CONCLUSION: ART CAN HEAL

Kipling faced many traumas and dramas, from a poor foster care experience to family drama to the death of his children. Still, he kept his faith, and he kept on writing. Like all the writers we've explored so far, Kipling stands for resilience in a way that forces us to pause and remember just how important it is to keep on going, and how creating art can not only bring purpose and meaning into your life, but can also heal.

ROBERT FROST - PART 1

This Chapter is titled *Robert Frost, Part 1,* because Frost is a journey to discover. With several homes from varying years of his life to explore, Frost is an epic New England pilgrimage. For *Rebel Writers Vol I,* we will explore the *Robert Frost Stone House Museum* in Shaftsbury, Vermont. Shaftsbury is also where Frost's final resting place is. We will revisit other Frost homes in future volumes.

* * *

UPON ARRIVING at the *Robert Frost Stone House Museum,* the first thing that resonated with me was how peaceful it was. Also, since I've been to his Derry, New Hampshire farm twice, I wanted to familiarize myself with the time of Frost's life when he lived in Shaftsbury. Where was he in his career at that moment? What was his daily life like? After all, this is the place he wrote the famous *Stopping by Woods on a Snowy Evening*. Here's what I learned.

* * *

THE DETAILS

1. Robert Frost's mother, Isabelle Frost, often read to her children from the Bible and shared stories from her homeland of Scotland. Apparently, until the age of 14, Frost never read a book all the way through by himself.

2. Child Frost also wasn't a fan of school. He often complained about stomachaches and didn't want to go. He spent some time homeschooled, but when he learned he could play sports in high school, he decided he'd give going in person a try. It was there that he became an avid reader, honor student, editor of his high school newspaper, started writing poetry, and fell in love with his future wife, Elinor White.

3. Elinor and Robert graduated in 1892 as co-valedictorians of their class. Both loved poetry. After high school, they were secretly engaged, planning to marry after college graduation. Things took a turn, however, when Robert left college before the first semester and asked Elinor to marry him right away instead. But Elinor made him wait. In fact, she made him wait three full years while she finished school. The two high school sweethearts finally wed in 1895. They were married over 40 years until her death in 1938. Elinor was his muse. Her later death was one of many tragedies for Frost.

4. Elinor and Robert had six children, however, not all survived. Their first son died because of infant cholera at 3 ½. It's believed that this tragedy is likely tied to his poem "Home Burial." Their surviving children were born between

1899-1905. The children mostly grew up on the Derry Farm in New Hampshire until Frost sold it. Which brings us to #5.

5. There's a fabulous interview of Frost that was done around 1952, which I found on *You Tube* after my visit (you can watch it too, as it's listed in the bibliography). In it, Frost explains how, while he was never "discouraged" by American publishers, he was never "encouraged" either. *So, he took a chance, sold his Derry home, and moved the entire family to England.* He planned to write a novel to get the family back on its feet. When he got there, he spread his poems out on the floor and realized he had enough for a book. A publisher agreed and published his first poetry collection, *A Boy's Will.* Frost later moved back to America in 1915 when the family became home sick. It's said that the family set out to find a home where they could "live cheap and get Yankier and Yankier." They settled on a home in Franconia, New Hampshire, where they lived before coming to Vermont.

6. It wasn't until 1920 that the Frost family came to the *Stone House* in Vermont. By this time, one of his children was working in New York, another had finished high school and wanted to farm. His two youngest were finishing up high school. Frost generously deeded the house to his son- and daughter-in-law, with the caveat that the entire Frost family could continue living there while the last two children completed high school.

7. As I noted, the *Stone House* is the famous house where Frost wrote *Stopping by Woods on a Snowy Evening*. I always imagined he wrote this in the middle of a New England

winter, however, that's not true at all! While Frost experienced the moment he wrote about, during the bitter cold winter months, he didn't write the poem right away. The image of that moment stayed with him, so he finally jotted it down in June at his dining room table. If you visit the *Stone House,* you too can stand in that space—both outside on his property and inside, where he wrote the poem.

8. Something that resonated with me at the *Stone House* was the record player that plays Frost reading his poetry on loop in the dining room. There was also, at least during my visit, a Virtual Reality Exhibit where you can experience, *Stopping by Woods on a Snowy Evening*. Both the albums and the virtual reality experience was amazing, but to be honest, I enjoyed just soaking up the liminal space where Frost once sat crafting his poetry the most.

9. Frost never had a desk or office space. He liked to write wherever, except outside, because, well, according to Frost in the 1952 interview, outside you have to deal with bugs.

10. At the *Stone House,* there is a gorgeous walk around the property that connects various postings of his poems to the nature that inspired them, including the "Mending Wall."

SOME OTHER HIGHLIGHTS? There is a self-guided tour full of Frost's items, including his spectacles and various books on display. Outside, you can also hang out on the Adirondack chairs, to soak up up the gorgeous yard. I took this as an opportunity to write some Frost inspired poetry. There is something magical about writing in the same space that Frost once spent his time (even if he didn't enjoy writing outside, I didn't mind it one bit).

HERE'S a poem I crafted in Frost's yard:

Remember
By: Sarah Crowne

Remember!
To be alive!
The sun hot
The birds bold
The moment NOW.

The sky stretched wide and blue
Whispering of something true.
While hose sprayed rainbows
Leave drops of glass on grass
Like morning dew.

Oh, to remember
To be alive
Living loud.

For the world may quarrel
But let no such quarrel reach your heart.

KEY REFLECTIONS

1. YOU DON'T NEED FANCY THINGS TO MAKE DREAMS COME TRUE

Frost didn't have a solid writing space, he wrote wherever

and whenever he was inspired. Today, especially with social media, so many of us are busy giving tours of our spectacular workspaces, which, I know, is fun but can lead one to thinking they need something "extra" to do their work. That's simply not true. As we saw with Twain and Alcott, who both wrote at tiny desks, bigger doesn't equal better. I am writing this at my kitchen counter. The glorious thing about writing is you can do it anywhere and on anything if you had to. In fact, sometimes, writing in notebooks and scrap pieces of paper makes one more inspired. The same can hold true for any passion. While tools and spaces are helpful, be sure to focus on the things you need to get something done. If you want it bad enough, you'll find a way.

2. TAKE A CHANCE

Frost took a chance when he moved to England. He packed up his entire family, setting off to a country where he did not know if it was going to be the right decision. I can't help but wonder, if he hadn't gone to England, would we still have Frost's poetry today? Was it this move that set off his career? Or maybe it would have just looked different. The point is, he took a chance, and that chance ended up leading him on a journey even he didn't expect.

3. PLANS CAN CHANGE

When Frost set out to England, he planned to write a novel. It wasn't until he got there that he realized he had enough poems to make a poetry book. It's interesting that it took this change of scenery for him to realize this. I presume he had the same number of poems in New Hampshire? Yet, it took a major move for him to realize what was special about him all along- his poetry. Frost wasn't afraid, despite the big move, to change his plans and go with the poetry book instead. Though I can't help but wonder what reading a Frost novel would be like!

CONCLUSION: TAKE A CHANCE ON YOU

Frost led so many adventures and faced multiple tragedies. As noted, we will continue to explore Frost in future volumes of *Rebel Writers*. That said, exploring the Frost Stone House Museum provided me with quiet solitude, soaking up everything Frost from his dining room table to his apple orchard outside. It reminded me what it means to be a writer, or any dream seeker. Taking a chance on yourself is the number one lesson we all take from Frost and all the great historic writers. They all took a chance, even when no one else believed in their work.

HERMAN MELVILLE

I confess: when I visited Herman Melville's home, Arrowhead, in Pittsfield, Massachusetts, I had never read *Moby Dick: Or, The White Whale*. I came with little knowledge on Melville himself, yet I left not only inspired but with a copy of *Moby Dick* to which I would later find is a beloved treasure. Upon the first line, "Call me Ishmael," I couldn't put it down. I expected to be bogged down by the language, being a historic novel. I'd been warned by other readers of the long narratives regarding whaling history that they claimed interrupted the narrative drive. But I was hooked from page one, enthralled in the historical tale that often made me feel like I was time traveling, while also finding the resonance of the human spirit and struggles of modern day wrapped within it at the same time. What made the reading experience even better? Having visited Arrowhead, where I learned so many surprises about this author.

* * *

I VISITED Arrowhead on a warm fall day as the leaves were just beginning to turn. The home itself is a gold-colored colonial house built in 1785, complete with its original barn. Melville lived here from 1850 to 1863, which was also some of his most productive writing years. While living at Arrowhead, Melville wrote major works including *Moby Dick*, *Pierre*, *The Confidence Man*, *Israel Potter*, and *The Piazza Tales* (which is a short story collection named for Arrowhead's porch!). Originally, the home was a farmhouse and inn, also next to Melville's uncle's property. After visiting his uncle's home several times, Melville decided he would borrow money to purchase the land next door. According to my tour guide, his uncle moved shortly after Melville's purchase.

THE DETAILS

1. Melville was born on August 1, 1819, in New York City. He was the third child of Allan and Maria Gansevoort Melvill (I believe the "e" in Melville came later). Eventually, his family would consume of four boys and four girls.

2. Melville's grandfather was Major Thomas Melville, a member of the Boston Tea Party in 1773. Thus, Melville had a revolutionary pedigree as his paternal grandfather participated in the Boston Tea Party and served as a Major in General Washington's army. His maternal grandfather, General Peter Gansevoort, was famous for leading the defense of Fort Stanwix in upstate New York against the British.

3. A young Melville loved to read. He especially loved Shakespeare, mythology, anthropology and history. It's

believed that he also grew up hearing about the whale-ship Essex, which was attached by a whale and sunk when Melville was just a year old. Sadly, in 1826, Melville came down with Scarlet Fever, which left him with weakened eyesight.

4. Melville's father supported the family by importing French dry goods. His business decision to try his luck at the fur business proved to be a failure. Within two short years, Melville's family was bankrupt, and his father died, leaving his mother a widow with eight children under the age of 17. The family then moved from high society New York City to New York state to make ends meet. It was after his father's death that the "e" was added to "Melville."

5. Melville and his older brother left school to work, to help support the family. He worked various jobs that ranged from banking to teaching school. He even studied surveying and engineering.

6. While Melville began writing at a young age, the disparities of his family's financial woes significantly affected him. Much of Melville's youth was a quest for security. When an opportunity to work at the Erie Canal project fell through, Melville's journey on a ship came to be. Working as a cabin boy on the *St Lawrence,* which was a merchant ship that sailed out of New York City in June 1839 for Liverpool. When he returned, his family was still in financial despair. After varying jobs, including teaching, in which the school closed without paying him, Melville ended up sailing on the

whaler ship, called *Acushnet* from New Bedford, Massachusetts to the South Seas.

7. The *Acushnet* traveled to the Marquesas Islands, which is present day French Polynesia. It was here that Melville and a companion jumped ship and spent four months as guest-captives of a supposed cannibalistic Typee people, which became the subject of his first novel, *Typee* (1846). Then, he eventually sought rescue on the Australia whale-ship Lucy Ann, where he traveled to Tahiti.

In Tahiti, his journey took an unusual turn when both he and his crew committed mutiny by refusing their duty. After being briefly jailed, Melville escaped to a nearby island where he worked on a potato farm. But the adventure didn't stop there! He eventually ending up joining the crew of whaler, *Charles and Henry,* working as a harpooner. For five months, he also even worked as a clerk and bookkeeper at a general store in Honolulu. Then, he enlisted in the US Navy and embarked on the rest of his journey, working as a seaman on a Navy Ship through the Pacific. He returned home in October 1844, ready to write about his adventures.

8. Melville, his wife Lizzie, and their young song vacationed in the Berkshires during the summer of 1850. During the visit, Melville met none other than Nathanial Hawthorne. The two became fast friends while attending the same picnic at Monument Mountain in Pittsfield. After Melville purchased the farm, he would name Arrowhead, after digging up multiple arrows on the land during planting season.

Melville and Hawthorne continued their friendship. The tour guide told me they used to hang out in the barn to smoke and swear because such behavior wasn't allowed inside the house (or as Hawthorne is said to have written in his diary, that they would talk deep into the night about "time and eternity, things of this world and of the next, and books, and publishers, and all possible and impossible matter"). Hawthorne even had his own bedroom off of Melville's study for when he sometimes stayed over. Melville found great inspiration in Hawthorne, and in fact, he dedicated *Moby Dick* to him.

9. Melville's mother and two of his sisters lived at Arrowhead with Melville, his wife, and children. Though he was a best-selling author when he began writing *Moby Dick, Moby Dick* did not see success. First published in the United Kingdom in October 1851, many reviewers trashed it. It sold fewer than 4000 copies in total and was out of print when Melville died. It wasn't until the 1920s, long after Melville's death, that the book gained recognition.

10. Sadly, Melville ended up having to sell Arrowhead to his brother when he could no longer afford it. He spent the last 25 years of his life out of the public eye and stopped writing novels. He wrote poetry every day. After a series of illnesses, he died at age 72 in Manhattan. Even more tragically, his oldest son Malcom shot himself, though there is debate about whether it was intentional or an accident. It is believed that he had argued with Melville the night before. His youngest son, Stanwix, died of tuberculosis in 1886.

During the tour, I was able to visit Melville's study. The window in front of his desk faces Mount Greylock. I couldn't help but imagine Melville there, writing *Moby Dick* as he looked out at that mountain. Herman Melville is long gone from this earth, but Mount Greylock and the words he wrote still stand.

KEY REFLECTIONS

1. FRIENDS ARE IMPORTANT. Especially friends that share your passions. Hawthorne and Melville shared a passion for the universe, for mysteries of this life and the next, for stories that would move the world. From their picnic meeting to their late night talks and smoking and swearing in the barn . . . their friendship inspired them both, proving that it is necessary in this life to share and confer your passions with other creative people. Friends are hard to come by, so if you find one, keep them and encourage them so that the world can be filled with great art and great friendship.

3. LIFE WON'T ALWAYS MAKE SENSE. I am sure it was daunting and heartbreaking for Melville to dedicate such time and care to *Moby Dick* to then only witness it flop. Surely, at least I hope, he knew he'd written a masterpiece. But the world is not always ready for your work. You can never predict how your work will prevail in your life, or after. Write it anyway. Create it anyway. Dream anyway. Without dreams, who are we as human beings? *Moby Dick* may not have been a commercial success, but it is a human success that has proven to inspire generations and will do so for years to come.

4. KEEP LEARNING. Melville remained curious and continued to learn, even though his education was cut short. He was a voracious reader who educated himself on a wide range of subjects. From philosophy to history, literature and science, he never let his intellectual curiosity cease. As he wrote in *Moby Dick*, "A whale-ship was my Yale College and my Harvard." You can do anything, even with limited resources, if you dedicate the time.

CONCLUSION: PURSUE MEANING

Melville pursued the meaning and truth of life, in both his real-life adventures from working odd jobs, to sailing the world, to writing alone in his study, overlooking Greylock Mountain. Even if he stopped writing novels, he continued to explore the human spirit in poetry. Melville teaches us that no matter what our failures or tragedies, we should always push on, pursuing truth in our human experience. We should never stop dreaming, never stop asking questions, and always have the courage to continue our journeys, no matter where they take us.

HARRIET BEECHER STOWE

Born on June 14, 1811, in Litchfield, Connecticut, Harriett Beecher Stowe was the seventh child of Congregational minister, Lyman Beecher and his wife, Roxana Foote Beecher. Most widely known as the author of the best-selling anti-slavery novel, *Uncle Tom's Cabin,* Harriett's writing career spanned 51 years. In fact, she published over 30 books, including *New England Sketches* (1835) and *The Mayflower: Sketches of Scenes and Characters among the Descendants of the Pilgrim* (1843), as well as multiple poems, hymns, short stories and articles.

* * *

I VISITED the Harriet Beecher Stowe Center in Hartford, Connecticut. It was unlike any other tour I've taken. As part of the tour, all guests sat together in Harriet's parlor for a discussion on current events and how they relate to Harriet's works and life. In a world that often feels choked by division, I found this experience both positive and inspiring as guests and tour guides, of diverse ethnic, religious, and financial backgrounds, sat together to discuss current events and how they relate to Harriet's work and legacy. It reminded me that while there will always be differences of opinions; it is important that we offer one another compassion, empathy, and understanding.

THE DETAILS

1. Harriet's home, which is now the Harriet Beecher Stowe Center, is next door to Mark Twain's house (Remember, from Chapter One, they were neighbors!). Twain visited Harriet here. It's said that they discussed publishing when he came.

2. The home was a downsize for Harriet. She had a much larger mansion prior, which no longer exists.

3. People consider Harriet the first "Snowbird" because she had homes in both Connecticut and Florida. You can visit the Mandarin Museum and Historical Society in Jacksonville, Florida (which I hope to visit myself for future volumes of *Rebel Writers*) to learn more about her time there.

Fun Fact: According to the tour guide, Harriet had her staff package and ship all her furniture each year to the Florida home because she didn't want to buy two sets of furniture. That must have been a lot of work!

4. Harriet was the daughter of the prominent Congregationalist minister, Lyman Beecher, and Roxana

Foote Beecher. All seven of her brothers became preachers. Her sister Catherine was a pioneer or education for young woman, and her sister Isabelle was the founder of the National Women's Suffrage Association. Harriet was certainly part of a remarkable family for its time.

5. Harriet's mother died when Harriet was just five years old. This would be the first of many tragedies for Harriet. Her mother's death affected the entire family, including her eldest sister, Catherine, who was thrust into the role of caring for her younger siblings. Harriet's father did eventually remarry, having three more children with his new wife.

6. According to the tour guide, the family was known as the "Beecher Preachers." Also, their father encouraged all the children to speak and learn about the social issues of their time. He would gather the siblings at the dining room table, where they would write and comment on various social issues, in addition to sharing bible quotes. They did this by passing around a paper, each writing their thoughts on it, before passing the paper to the next person, who would add their thoughts as well. If you visit the museum, you can see a copy of this historical "group chat."

7. Harriet had many passions. First, she exhibited a passion for writing at a young age. At just seven years old, she won a contest for her writing. She was also an artist, just like her mother. The home displays several of Harriet's floral paintings. Additionally, Harriet was a teacher. In fact, she was both a student and a teacher at the Hartford Female Seminary, which was founded by her sister Catherine.

. . .

8. At 21 years old, Harriet moved with her family to Cincinnati, Ohio. It was there that she met her husband, Calvin Stowe. Harriet and Calvin met at the informal writer's club called the "Semi-Colon Club." According to the tour guide, Harriet's best friend Eliza also attended the club and was married to Calvin. It was after Eliza's death that Harriet and Calvin became romantically involved. He kept Eliza's portrait hanging in his study, even after marrying Stowe and having several children with her. One of their daughter's names was Eliza. There is also a character named Eliza in *Uncle Tom's Cabin.*

9. Harriett gave birth to seven children. Sadly, her infant son died of cholera at eighteen months. Another son drowned in the Connecticut River while attending college at age nineteen. A third son disappeared after moving to San Francisco after serving for the Union in the Civil War. It's said that Harriet often had seances in the parlor of the Hartford home, as she worried her children hadn't made it to heaven and wanted confirmation.

10. Harriet wrote *Uncle Tom's Cabin* at age 39, while performing domestic duties, raising children, and amidst great despair and grief. It's thought that many of the tragedies she'd experienced, especially the loss of her infant son, inspired the novel. The grief, combined with having witnessed an African American woman being separated from her child during a slave auction in Kentucky, fueled her passion for the story.

. . .

11. Harriet first wrote *Uncle Tom's Cabin* as a short story for the abolitionist newspaper, *The National Era*. The newspaper loved it so much, it asked for more. Harriet obliged by sending more chapters. Eventually, the newspaper published almost the entire novel! Harriet, however, in marketing genius, left the last chapter out so readers would buy the book.

12. *Uncle Tom's Cabin* was officially published as a full novel in 1852, in two volumes. It sold 10,000 copies in its first week! But that was just the beginning. It later sold 300,000 copies during its first year of publication, and in Great Britain, 1.5 million copies. During the 19th century, the only book to outsell *Uncle Tom's Cabin* was the Bible. Today, the novel is translated into more than 70 languages and is sold throughout the world.

13. Harriet made her case against slavery in *Uncle Tom's Cabin*. She also later published a collection of documents and testimony titled, *A Key to Uncle Tom's Cabin* in 1853 because many critics wanted "proof" of the novel's representation of slavery.

It is important to note that the novel is not without criticism. While some praise the novel for its impact on bringing the harsh realities of slavery to light, others criticize it for its use of stereotypes and limited views. Harriet was familiar with first-hand accounts of slavery. Both her husband and her brother helped shelter a man and helped with the informal underground railroad. She also employed at least one fugitive in her home.

. . .

14. Harriet was fiercely against slavery. While there is some controversy regarding the idea that she did not do enough to stop slavery after writing *Uncle Tom's Cabin*, she did donate money towards the antislavery cause. She also helped establish schools for African American children in Florida.

15. Harriet died on July 1, 1896, at noon in her Hartford home. Despite the controversies surrounding her work, it is undeniable that she showed immense courage writing and publishing *Uncle Tom's Cabin*. This powerful novel began a conversation about one of the most horrific injustices in human history. Harriet's passionate depiction of the inhumanity and cruelty of slavery set fire to widespread awareness, igniting debate and a powerful movement against it.

KEY REFLECTIONS

1. YOU CAN BALANCE MULTIPLE ROLES

Harriet was a mom to seven children and still wrote over 30 books! Not only that, she continued to contribute to society by standing up for her beliefs as she toured both nationally and internationally to raise awareness to end slavery. While she had help (she employed servants at her home), her steadfast tenacity is an inspiring example that you can do the things you are passionate about with steadfast determination.

2. YOU CAN TURN PERSONAL STRUGGLES INTO MOTIVATION

From losing her mother to her 18-month-old son and other tragedies, Harriet used her grief to fuel her work. Her ability to transform personal pain into a powerful force for change inspires us to see that even in hardship, we can find the strength to make a difference in the world. Our struggles do not define us, they empower us. We can use our struggles to empower and help others, too.

3. CHANGE STARTS WITH ORDINARY PEOPLE

Harriet shows us that ordinary people can have an extraordinary impact on society. In a time when a woman's voice was not always heard, she used her voice on a controversial subject that was brewing up to a civil war. Harriet's life encourages us to see that we can use our talents and experiences, no matter the circumstances, to contribute and facilitate meaningful change in the world, no matter how hard that task is.

CONCLUSION: STORIES HOLD INCREDIBLE POWER

Overall, Harriet's life showed me that each of our voices holds not only incredible power, but that we can transform our personal challenges into opportunities. She used her voice for the power of storytelling to not only raise awareness, but to contribute to the fight against one of the greatest injustices of her time. She is indeed a clear example of how the power of story can impact others.

BEING A REBEL WRITER

I started this journey looking for adventure. Inspiration. Something to unlock the block I was feeling. A way to navigate through this life of seeing the world in lines and stanzas, stories that haunted and begged to be told. Like any good detective, I went on an investigation of sorts, trying to uncover the root of what it means to be a writer, a creative soul that wants to leave some positive imprint on the world.

What I found surprised me. My lack of understanding what it means to be a writer wasn't stalling me. It wasn't a shortage of adventure either (life is an adventure, after all). It was fear.

Writing itself is an act of bravery. To have the courage to write your thoughts, your feelings, your dreams is to take back your power, your voice. In today's argumentative cancel culture, it's even more intimidating. We are secretly counting the cost of speaking out, even if it's just sharing a sentence on our love of books, warm weather, or whatever it might be. Someone, somewhere, out there, is going to criticize it.

What I learned is that this doesn't mean we shouldn't

write. It doesn't mean we shouldn't put down our stories, express our hearts in song or art. It shouldn't stop us from daring to dream and create. We also shouldn't create to meet a status quo, or try to predict whatever the "next big thing" is. We should create because we need to. Because sharing our stories teaches us what it means to be human. It's necessary for human connection and growth. Imagine a world without Frost's poems? Lovecraft's weird fiction? A world with no lessons from Melville's whale, no anti-slavery novel by Stowe?

What about more modern stories we know today? Think of the books, the movies, the music, the art that has inspired you. The ones that brought you comfort in hard times or taught you something you didn't know. Or even just the ones that made you smile, laugh, or dance. Where would we be without stories? At its root, every song, even instrumental, every movie, every book, every piece of art, every life, has a story behind it.

Stories are necessary for the human experience. Bravery is necessary to not only write them, but live them.

When I started writing this book, I debated on a title. Originally, it was called "A Write Life" because my journey was to discover what the "write life" really meant. However, once I'd visited the last home on my list for this first volume, I quickly changed it to Rebel Writers. Why? Because I realized after doing everything from standing on Twain's porch to staring out at the train tracks that inspired Warner, to feeling the cool, crisp air of Kipling's Vermont and Melville's Greylock Mountain and all the adventures in between-that each of these writers were rebels. They wrote the stories that taunted them, sometimes doing so while dealing with past traumas, poverty, poor health, amid self-doubt, and in eras that weren't always ready for the stories they had to tell. Still, they set forth, brave. They unleashed the genius behind the pen, taking a chance, even despite their failures.

To me, that's a rebel. A person who isn't afraid to speak their truth with the hopes it will somehow bring healing, hope and love to others in this world and the next because human spirit, human connection, human stories - those are the threads that bind us eternally.

I set off looking for an adventure. I wanted to uncover the secrets of the great historical writers. Instead, I found a lesson I knew from the start.

Let me tell you the story that helped me become brave.

* * *

THE STORY

The Soldier and The Sandbags

Once upon a time, there was a soldier in the Vietnam war. One scorching hot day, he decided to fill his squad's tank with sandbags. Everyone made fun of him. They said, "Man, why are you doing that? It's a waste of time. It's too hot today!" But the man ignored them and kept filling the tank with sandbags anyway, all by himself. Sandbag after sandbag in the jungle heat.

Later that day, as the soldiers ventured out into the trials of war, the tank blew when it hit a minefield. And guess what? The shards of glass that would have killed the soldiers went into the sandbags instead, saving them all. The man, while knocked unconscious and blown out of the tank, survived, along with the others.

In fact, the soldier that filled the tank with sandbags also rescued each man still inside the tank, one by one, when he came to. He received a Purple Heart for his heroic efforts.

That man was my father.

. . .

HOW IT MADE ME BRAVE

My parents separated when I was young. I didn't always know this story. I am saddened to say there were times in my childhood when I didn't see my father. It didn't help matters that my dad lived in a camp trailer in the middle of the woods for a time. I thought it was so weird. I didn't want my friends to know my dad lived in this camper. I felt embarrassed. I was angry he'd left. I didn't understand the traumas and things war does to a man.

I reunited with my father as a young adult after some trials and back and forth in that process. We had many good years, rebuilding our relationship.

Still, I didn't know the story of the sandbags. My father didn't talk about Vietnam much. I got pieces of the story, sure. But it wasn't until after he died that I learned it all. Or should I say, it was only then that it really sunk in.

My revelation was this: My dad bet on himself. Because he bet on himself, he lived on and so did the men in his platoon. Despite all the naysayers, he trusted himself and kept going. Because he did that, I'm alive today. And so are my children.

Likewise, you need to bet on you. We're all fighting wars. We're all trying to find ourselves, accomplish our dreams, discover our way through life.

Every writer I wrote about in this book bet on themselves, too.

They were brave. They were rebels. Despite what anyone else said or thought, they always bet on themselves.

So be brave. Bet on you.

You'll be so thankful you did. And so will the threads of time as your gifts to the world shape and inspire generations to come.

Now, get out there and make your dreams come true!

A COLLECTION OF LESSONS FROM REBEL WRITERS

Here's a roundup of key lessons from these brave writers.

1. Life is an Adventure

Twain taught us life is an adventure. He didn't just write about adventures; he lived them. We can find adventure each day if we look for it. Go find your adventure!

2. Fight for Your Dreams

Alcott never gave up on her dreams. Remember her tiny desk? Long hours switching hands to write? She did it while living in poverty. I'm so thankful she did.

3. Always Be You

Hawthorne stayed true to his artistic vision, often resisting to conform to the literary trends of his time. Don't let the world dictate your voice, use your own.

. . .

4. Tell Your Story, No Matter How Weird

Lovecraft reminded us you should always tell your story, no matter how weird. You never know who may need to hear it or how it may heal or inspire others.

5. When You Put Your Passions First, You Can Accomplish Anything

Warner showed us you can have more than one passion. She was both a beloved schoolteacher and an exceptional writer. You can do or be more than one thing. Try new things and don't limit yourself. There are endless possibilities when you step outside of your comfort zone.

6. Art Can Heal You

From a poor foster care experience to family drama to the death of his children, Kipling faced many traumas throughout his life. Still, he kept his faith, and he kept on writing. Writing can heal us as we use it as a tool to not only overcome our own ghosts, but to stand bravely to share our stories with others to help them face theirs too.

7. Take a Chance

Frost took a chance when he moved his family to England, hoping to write the next great novel. Instead, he realized he had enough poems already for a poetry book. Still, it was the act of moving to England that helped open him up to seeing what he already had. Don't let fear hold you back from exploring new opportunities.

. . .

8. Pursue Meaning

Melville never stopped pursuing meaning. From his real-life sailing adventures to working odd jobs to writing poetry later in life, he kept learning and exploring. Melville shows us that no matter what our failures are, we should always move forward, learning from our experiences.

9. Story Holds Incredible Power

Stowe reminds us that our voices and the stories they tell hold incredible power. Think about the stories you want to write, and the impact you want to make on the world.

10. Bet On You

Last but not least, my own discoveries of the importance of "betting on yourself" teach us that to move forward in life, we must take chances and believe in ourselves. Like Dorothy in The Wizard of Oz, you've always had the power. Now use it.

THE JOURNEY IS JUST GETTING STARTED

I'm still out there touring historic writers' homes! Ralph Waldo Emerson, Henry David Thoreau, Emily Dickinson, Edith Wharton, Noah Webster, and more . . . all coming in future volumes of *Rebel Writers*! It's going to be epic!

If this book has inspired you or if you'd like to recommend a historic writer's home to explore, please reach out to me at whatsgoinonslnpublishing@gmail.com.

Till then, keep creating, keep dreaming, and never give up!

XOXO,

Sarah Crowne

BIBLIOGRAPHY

Mark Twain

Biography.com Editors. "Mark Twain – Quotes, Books & Real Name." *Biography*, 31 Mar. 2021, www.biography.com/authors-writers/mark-twain. Accessed 23 September 2024.

Maloney, Wendi A. "This Day in History: Mark Twain Debuts Iconic Style at Library of Congress Timeless." *The Library of Congress*, 7 Dec. 2017, blogs.loc.gov/loc/2017/12/this-day-in-history-mark-twain-debutes-iconic-style-at-library-of-congress/. Accessed 23 September 2024.

"Mark Twain Biography & Facts." *Encyclopedia Britannica*, www.britannica.com/biography/Mark-Twain. Accessed 23 Sept. 2024.

"Mark Twain's Daughters – Hartford Courant." *Courant.com*, 2020, digitaledition.courant.com/tribune/article_popover.aspx?guid=ab9d740d-d8e7-4515-9dbe96660f4026b5. Accessed 23 September 2024.

"The Mark Twain House." *Mark Twain House*, marktwainhouse-.org/about/the-house/HartfordHome/. Accessed 23 Sept. 2024.

Powers, Ron. *Mark Twain.* Simon and Shuster, 20 Sept. 2005.

Wilbers, Helen. "The Many Friendships of Mark Twain." *Fultonsun.com, Fulton Su*, 18 Feb. 2021, www.fultonsun.com/news/2021/feb/18/many-friendships-mark-twain/. Accessed 23 September 2024.

Louisa May Alcott

Croucher, Kalvin. "8 Things You Might Not Have Known about Louisa May Alcott." *Well Read Company USA*, Well Read Company USA, 14 Mar. 2024, https://us.wellreadcompany.com/blogs/well-read-company-blog/8-things-you-might-not-have-known-about-louisa-may-alcott?srsltid=AfmBOorOBRKnc8Ax4Rgljvp1QyutKm-JOddJ9J6jeUklJIo0d1eNuO81. Accessed 24 September 2024.

House, Louisa May Alcott's Orchard. "Welcome to " the Home of Little Women" ... And so Much More." Louisa May Alcott's Orchard House, louisamayalcott.org. Accessed 24 September 2024.

"7 Surprising Facts about Louisa May Alcott | MASTERPIECE." Masterpiece, 2017, www.pbs.org/wgbh/masterpiece/specialfeatures/little-women-7-surprising-facts-about-louisa-may-alcott/. Accessed 24 September 2024.

Norwood, Arlisha R. "Louisa May Alcott." National Women's History Museum, 2017, www.womenshistory.org/education-resources/biographies/louisa-may-alcott Accessed 24 Sept. 2024.

"Walking through the House Where Louisa May Alcott Wrote Little Women." Literary Hub, 2 Dec. 2019, lithub.com/walking-through-the-house-where-louisa-may-alcott-wrote-little-women/. Accessed 24 Sept. 2024.

NATHANIEL HAWTHORNE

Britannica. "Nathaniel Hawthorne | American Writer." Encyclopedia Britannica, 30 June 2018, www.britannica.com/biography/Nathaniel-Hawthorne. Accessed 25 Sept. 2024.

Cole, Lester, et al. "The House of the Seven Gables." IMDb, 12 Apr. 1940, www.imdb.com/title/tt0032610/. Accessed 25 Sept. 2024.

interGen support. "Scarlet Letter (Hawthorne)." Litlovers.com, 2024, litlovers.com/reading-guides/fiction/scarlet-letter-hawthorne?showall=1#google_vignette. Accessed 25 Sept. 2024.

"Nathaniel Hawthorne, Salem, Massachusetts, House of Seven Gables | Literary Traveler." Literary Traveler | Explore Your Literary Imagination, 16 July 2005, www.literarytraveler.com/articles/hawthorne_salem_ma/. Accessed 25 Sept. 2024.

Poets, Academy of American. "About Nathaniel Hawthorne | Academy of American Poets." Poets.org, poets.org/poet/nathaniel-hawthorne. Accessed 25 Sept. 2024.

yesterdaysamerica. "Author Spotlight: Nathaniel Hawthorne." Yesterday's America, 19 July 2023, yesterdaysamerica.com/author-spotlight-nathaniel-hawthorne/. Accessed 25 Sept. 2024.

Hawthorne birthplace - the House of the Seven Gables. (n.d.). The House of the Seven Gables. https://7gables.org/archives-category/hawthorne-birthplace/. Accessed October 6, 2024.

H.P. LOVECRAFT

HPLHS – the H.P. Lovecraft Historical Society. (n.d.) https://www.hplhs.org/. Accessed October 1, 2024.

Lovecraft Arts & Sciences (n.d.). LOVECRAFT ARTS & SCIENCES. https://www.weirdprovidence.org. Accessed October 3, 2024.

The Arcade Providence, Providence, RI 02903. (n.d.). https://www.visitrhodeisland.com/listing/the-arcade-providence/9116/. Accessed October 1, 2024.

The Editors of Encyclopedia Britannica. (2024, August 16). *H.P. Lovecraft biography, Books, & Facts.* Encyclopedia Britannica. https://www.britannica.com/biography/H-P-Lovecraft.

The H.P. Lovecraft Archive. (n.d.). https://www.hplovecraft.com. Accessed October 1, 2024.

We can't ignore H.P. Lovecraft's white supremacy. (2020, October 20). Literary Hub. https://lithub.com/we-cant-ignore-h-p-lovecrafts-white-supremacy/. Accessed October 1, 2024.

GERTRUDE CHANDLER WARNER

Bulletin, R. C. F. B. N. (2017, January 28). HISTORICALLY SPEAKING: Gertrude Chandler Warner wrote inspiring children's books. *The Bulletin.* https://www.norwichbulletin.com/story/news/2017/01/28/historiclaly-speaking-gertrude-chandler-warner/22588673007. Accessed 27 Sept. 2024.

Museum, American Writers. "Get to Know Gertrude." *The American Writers Museum,* 22 June 2017, americanwritersmuseum.org/get-to-know-gertrude/. Accessed 27 Sept. 2024.

The Gertrude Chandler Warner Boxcar Children Museum. (n.d.). The Gertrude Chandler Warner Boxcar Children Museum. https://boxcarchildrenmuseum.com/. Accessed 27 Sept. 2024.

RUDYARD KIPLING

Martyris, N. (2015, September 25). When Rudyard Kipling's son went missing. *The New Yorker*. https://www.newyorker.com/books/page-turner/when-rudyard-kiplings-son-went-missing. Accessed 27 Sept. 2024.

Stewart, J. I. (2024, September 14). *Rudyard Kipling | Biography, Books, Poems, & Facts*. Encyclopedia Britannica. https://www.britannica.com/biography/Rudyard-Kipling. Accessed 27 Sept. 2024.

Rudyard Kipling - historic UK. (2023, December 2). Historic UK. https://www.historic-uk.com/CultureUK/Rudyard Kipling/. Accessed 27 Sept. 2024.

Rudyard Kipling - More than our childhoods. (2022, July 12). More Than Our Childhoods. https://www.morethanourchildhoods.org/stories/rudyard-kipling/. Accessed 27 Sept. 2024.

Kipling's Naulakha — The Landmark Trust USA. (n.d.). The Landmark Trust USA. https://landmarktrustusa.org/rudyard-kiplings-naulakha. Accessed 27 Sept. 2024.

ROBERT FROST

Bradley.Battin. (2024, April 4). *Robert Frost stone house Museum Vermont Tourism.* Vermont Tourism. https://vermontvacation.com/robert-frost-stone-house-museum/.

Gerber, P. L. (2024, September 18). *Robert Frost Biography, Childhood, Poems, Books, Awards, & Facts.* Encyclopedia Britannica. https://www.britannica.com/biography/Robert-Frost.

Manufacturing Intellect. (2019, December 2). *Robert Frost Interview + Poetry Reading (1952)* [Video]. YouTube. https://www.youtube.com/watch?v=2qwCEnkb2_E.

Stopping By Woods On a Snowy Evening. (2024, August 12). The Poetry Foundation. https://www.poetryfoundation.org/poems/42891/stopping-by-wods-on-a-snowy-evening.

HERMAN MELVILLE

Academy of American Poets. (n.d.). *Herman Melville.* Poets.org. https//poets.org/poet/herman-melville. Accessed October 3, 2024.

American Experience, PBS. (2017, September 9). The life of Herman Melville. *American Experience, PBS. https://www.pbs.org/wgbh/americanexperience/features/whaling-biography-herman-melville/.* Accessed October 3, 2024.

Berkshire County Historical Society. (2023, June 16). *Herman Melville, Berkshire Historical Society.* https://berkshirehistory.org/herman-melivlle-arrowhead/. Accessed October 3, 2024.

Herman Melville. (2024, August 20). The Poetry Foundation. https://www.poetryfoundation.org/poets/herman-melville. Accessed October 3, 2024.

Maxwell, D. (2024, September 24). *Herman Melville, Books Facts & Biography.* Encyclopedia Britannica. https://www.britannica.com/biography/Herman-Melville. Accessed October 3, 2024.

Popova, M. (2020, August 13). *Herman Melville on writing and his daily routine.* The Marginalian. https://www.themarginalian.org/2014/01/30/herman-melville-daily-routine/. Accessed October 3, 2024.

HARRIET BEECHER-STOWE

Biography: Harriet Beecher Stowe. (n.d.). Biography: Harriet Beecher Stowe. https://www.womenshistory.org/education-resources/biogra phies/harriet-beecher-stowe

Harriet Beecher Stowe (U.S. National Park Service). (n.d.). https://www.nps.gov/people/harriet-beecher-stowe.htm

Harriet Beecher Stowe. (n.d.). https://fcit.usf.edu/florida/lessons/stowe/stowe.htm

Kratz, J. (2019, March 4). *Harriet Beecher Stowe: a fighter for social justice.* Pieces of History. https://prologue.blogs.archives.gov/2019/03/08/harriet-beecher-stowe-a-fighter-for-social-justice/

Life. (n.d.). Harriet Beecher Stowe Center. https://www.harrietbeecher stowecenter.org/harriet-beecher-stowe/harriet-beecher-

(no title). (n.d.). https://www.mandarinmuseum.org/

The Editors of Encyclopedia Britannica. (2024c, September 10). *Uncle Tom's Cabin | Summary, Date, & Significance*. Encyclopedia Britannica. https://www.britannica.com/topic/Uncle-Toms-Cabin/Major-themes-and-influences

ACKNOWLEDGMENTS

I never dreamed my visits to historic author homes, shared at my Substack, *A Busy Lady,* would inspire so many! A huge thank you to my husband Dane, for coming with me on this journey and my children, Dana and Max, who continue to inspire me. There's no one else I'd rather be on this journey with.

Also to my writing friends who inspire me each day and reminded me I might just be on to something visiting historic writers' homes! The best writers support one another, and I am always grateful for the ones that inspire me. A special thank you to writing teacher, John Truby, whose philosophy class "Thinkers Bootcamp" inspired me to think deeper about my journey as both a writer and a human being.

Thank you to Kelsey Gietl for the cover design! Multi-talented, you too are a rebel writer!

Most of all, thank you to the numerous people who have inspired me along the way (all of which you can read in my acknowledgments of my novel, ALL THESE THREADS OF TIME). I continue to be inspired in this life by so many and couldn't possibly name them all.

Thank you to all the writers that came before me and those that will come after me. Your bravery in telling your stories will truly change the world by inspiring, teaching, reminding and reflecting on what it means to be human and live a wonderful life. Stories really do have the power to change the world, if you tell them.

A huge thank you to all the tour guides and nonprofit leaders that inspired me on this journey. You are all amazing, with so much history to share, and often, working as volunteers to keep the memory of these prominent writers alive. The world thanks you.

Thank you to all of my Substack followers, who continue to support my work.

Last, and certainly not least, thank you reader for taking a chance on this book. I hope you live your journey with bravery, then write about it.

XOXO,
Sarah Crowne

ABOUT THE AUTHOR

Sarah Crowne is an author, poet, mom, teacher, and lawyer that believes stories have the power to change the world! Author of the thrilling time travel murder mystery, ***ALL THESE THREADS OF TIME***, you can find out more about Sarah, her upcoming works, events, and other interesting stuff at her website here: https://sarahcrownebooks.com/or at her Substack, https://abusylady.substack.com/. You can also support Sarah's work by following her on social media or by leaving a book review.

ALSO BY SARAH CROWNE

ALL THESE THREADS OF TIME

TUNE IN (coming 2025)

REBEL WRITERS: THE GENIUS BEHIND THE PEN, VOL. II (coming 2025)

A BUSY LADY SUBSTACK - Historic writer tours, author interviews, and empowering posts to help you make your dreams come true! Check it out at https://abusylady.substack.com/.

Learn about other upcoming works and events at

https://sarahcrownebooks.com

www.ingramcontent.com/pod-product-compliance
Ingram Content Group UK Ltd.
Pitfield, Milton Keynes, MK11 3LW, UK
UKHW041820200726
13854UKWH00001BA/145